The *Wizard* Of Oz

C000005012

Wise Publications
part of The Music Sales Group

London/New York/Paris/Sydney/Copenhagen/Berlin/Madrid/Hong Kong/Tokyo

Published by
Wise Publications
14-15 Berners Street,
London W1T 3LJ, UK.

Exclusive Distributors:
Music Sales Limited
Distribution Centre, Newmarket Road,
Bury St Edmunds, Suffolk IP33 3YB, UK.
Music Sales Corporation
180 Madison Avenue, 24th Floor,
New York NY 10016, USA.
Music Sales Pty Limited
Units 3-4, 17 Willfox Street, Condell Park
NSW 2200, Australia.

Order No. AM1010273
ISBN 978-1-78305-877-8

Edited by Jenni Norey.
Music processed by Paul Ewers Music Design.
Photographs courtesy of FPG/Hulton Archive and Authenticated News/Archive Photos/Getty Images.

Printed in the EU.

Your Guarantee of Quality
As publishers, we strive to produce every book to the
highest commercial standards.
This book has been carefully designed to minimise awkward
page turns and to make playing from it a real pleasure.
Particular care has been given to specifying acid-free, neutral-sized paper
made from pulps which have not been elemental chlorine bleached.
This pulp is from farmed sustainable forests and was
produced with special regard for the environment.
Throughout, the printing and binding have been planned to
ensure a sturdy, attractive publication which should give years of enjoyment.
If your copy fails to meet our high standards,
please inform us and we will gladly replace it.

www.musicsales.com

Contents

*T*his classic 1939 MGM musical fantasy brought together Judy Garland, some spectacular sets and a selection of very memorable songs in an elaborate production that has since become one of the most famous films ever made.

Success was by no means assured at the time. Seventeen-year-old Judy Garland was a little too old for her role as the little Kansas farm girl Dorothy Gale, but she made the part her own anyway. MGM barely made its money back with the initial release, although the film went on to earn many millions in later years. The songs, though, by 'Yip' Harburg and Harold Arlen, sounded like winners from the start.

'Over The Rainbow' is sung by Dorothy some 6 minutes into the film. She has been having a bad day with a crabby neighbour but gets short shrift from her busy Aunt Em who briskly tells her to find a place 'where she won't get into any trouble'. The song, offered as a young girl's reverie about whether such an impossibly ideal place might actually exist, won an Academy Award and acquired unexpected resonances over the years.

The film's second song comes after a twister has hit the farm house and a window sash has hit Dorothy in the head, propelling her from the sepia Mid-West into Technicolor-drenched Munchkinland. Here her guide is Glinda, the Good Witch of the North, who coaxes the pint-sized Munchkins from their hiding places ('Come Out, Come Out, Wherever You Are') and reveals that the falling Kansas farm house has miraculously killed the Wicked Witch of the East, so making Dorothy an instant heroine. Dorothy protests ('It Really Was No Miracle') but celebrations ensue with 'Ding Dong The Witch Is Dead'. A welcoming medley from various Munchkin delegations follow: 'Lullaby League', 'Lollipop Guild', and 'We Welcome You To Munchkinland'. It is then revealed that a Wicked Witch of the West also exists ('worse than her dead sister') posing a new threat to Dorothy's safety. Protected by a pair of magic ruby slippers, Dorothy is tunefully advised to 'Follow The Yellow Brick Road' and informed 'You're Off To See The Wizard' as the Munchkins send her on her way to the distant Emerald City, where resides the fabled Wizard of Oz who may be able to help her to get back to Kansas.

Most of the remaining songs are there mainly to help move the plot along, the exceptions being the much-loved 'If I Only Had A Brain', 'If I Only Had A Heart' and 'If I Only Had The Nerve' — shortfalls musically lamented by three eccentric companions Dorothy meets on her journey, respectively the Scarecrow, the Tin Man and the Cowardly Lion.
When the trio emerges from a forbidding forest, they hear the disembodied 'Optimistic Voices (You're Out Of The Woods)' and on eventually reaching the Emerald City, they are treated to a rousingly patriotic number ('The Merry Old Land Of Oz') by its citizens. At barely one hour into the film and with 40 minutes still to go comes the final song, the now-emboldened Cowardly Lion's 'If I Were King Of The Forest'.

For the final reel Herbert Stothart's Academy Award-winning score artfully revisits the melodies of several songs already heard. There is a brief instrumental reprise of 'Over The Rainbow' when Dorothy finally awakes from her delirious dream to find herself back in sepia-tinted Kansas surrounded by the familiar faces of family and friends; faces that had been transplanted to some of the characters in her fantasy. The film ends with Dorothy's tremulous voice and Stothart's swooping score reminding us simply that 'There's no place like home'.

Over The Rainbow

Words by E.Y. Harburg
Music by Harold Arlen

8

Come Out, Come Out, Wherever You Are/
It Really Was No Miracle

Words by E.Y. Harburg
Music by Harold Arlen

name of the star. (Kan - sas, she says, is the name of the star.)

She brings you good news. Or,

have - n't you heard: When she fell out of Kan - sas a mi - ra - cle oc -

- curred.

It

Ding Dong The Witch Is Dead

Words by E.Y. Harburg
Music by Harold Arlen

molto rall.

MAYOR:
As

♩ = 70

May-or of the Munch-kin Cit - y, in the coun-ty of the Land of Oz, I

BARRISTER:

wel - come you most re - gal - ly. But we've got to ve - ri - fy it le - gal - ly to

18

Lullaby League/Lollipop Guild/
We Welcome You To Munchkinland

Words by E.Y. Harburg
Music by Harold Arlen

23

Follow The Yellow Brick Road/ You're Off To See The Wizard

Words by E.Y. Harburg
Music by Harold Arlen

If I Only Had A Brain

Words by E.Y Harburg
Music by Harold Arlen

If I Only Had A Heart

Words by E.Y. Harburg
Music by Harold Arlen

I hear a beat, how sweet! 3. Just to re - gis - ter e - mo - tion, jea - lou - sy, de - vo - tion and real - ly feel the part. I could stay young and chip - per and I'd lock it with a zip - per if I on - ly___ had a heart.

If I Only Had The Nerve/
We're Off To See The Wizard

Words by E.Y. Harburg
Music by Harold Arlen

Optimistic Voices
(You're Out Of The Woods)

Words by E.Y. Harburg
Music by Harold Arlen

The Merry Old Land Of Oz

Words by E.Y. Harburg
Music by Harold Arlen

If I Were King Of The Forest

Words by E.Y. Harburg
Music by Harold Arlen

123456789